# LOOKING AT LIGHT

by

## Robin Twiddy

# BookLife
## PUBLISHING

©2018
BookLife Publishing
King's Lynn
Norfolk PE30 4LS

A catalogue record for this book is available from the British Library.

ISBN: 978-1-78637-351-9

**Written by:**
Robin Twiddy

**Edited by:**
Kirsty Holmes

**Designed by:**
Gareth Liddington

**Photocredits:** All images are courtesy of Shutterstock.com.

Cover - Studio 37, Fotokostic, iravgustin, natrot, 2 - Witaya Proadtayakogool, 3 - rangizzz, 4 - shapovalphoto, 5 - Realstock, 6 - stockelements, 7 - Triff, 8 - Benevolente82, 9 - GrashAlex, SFIO CRACHO, 10 - altanaka, 11 - Alexander Penyushkin, 12 - Evgeniya Anikienko, 13 - Havoc, 14 - MilanB, 15 - Rohappy, 16 - 40 Steps Beyond, 17 - Joey_danuphol, 18 - BarvArt, 19 - Dipak Shelare, Freedom_Studio, PavelShynkarou, 20 - lucas nishimoto, 21 - Poly Liss, 22 - sukisameeh94, Khumthong, Albert999, 23 - Alexander Penyushkin, 24 - LVV

Images are courtesy of Shutterstock.com. With thanks to Getty Images, Thinkstock Photo and iStockphoto.

# CONTENTS

Words that look like **this** can be found in the glossary on page 24.

# LIGHT AND DARK

## IS IT LIGHT OR DARK OUTSIDE?

Light is very important. We need light to see the world around us. We have natural light from the Sun, and we can make light too. But what is it?

Something which makes light is called a light source. The Sun is a light source and so are the lights in your home and classroom. When there is little or no light from a light source, we say it is dark.

# DAY AND NIGHT

## WHAT IS THE BIGGEST DIFFERENCE BETWEEN DAY AND NIGHT?

During the day, the Sun is in the sky. This fills your part of the world with light. People can see much better during the day than at night because we use light to see.

The Sun is actually a big burning ball of gas in space – WOW!

# WHY IS IT DARK AT NIGHT?

Moonlight isn't made by the Moon! It is actually just sunlight bouncing off the moon.

The Earth spins round once a day. When your part of the world faces the Sun it is daytime for you. When the Earth turns around, you move away from the Sun, and it becomes night time.

7

# LIGHT IT UP

## WHAT DO YOU DO WHEN IT GETS DARK AND YOU CAN'T SEE...

You should always be very careful around candles. Fire spreads fast!

...Turn on the lights! Before electric lights were **invented**, people had to use candles and fires to light their houses. This could be messy, smelly and dangerous. Some things that make light also make heat and can catch fire!

Electric lights made lighting houses much safer, but the first types of lightbulbs got very hot. Some newer types of bulbs can make light without getting hot. These are much safer. Look around you: how many electric lights can you see?

Energy-saving light bulbs are better for the environment.

# SHADOWS

## HOW ARE SHADOWS MADE?

Light can pass through **transparent** materials such as glass or water. It bounces off things that are **opaque**, like wood – or you!

You will always be in between the light source and your shadow.

Shadows can be lots of fun. What shapes can you make?

Think about a shadow as the place where the light can't get to. Try holding your hand up in front of a torch in a dark room. Where is the shadow? Try moving the torch around. What happens to the shadow? Now try pointing two torches at the same object. What happens now?

# REFLECTIONS

Your reflection should go the same way as you do!

Mirrors are great for checking that you are looking cool. Shiny, smooth things, like glass or polished metal, reflect light. Try looking at yourself in a mirror. Now move to the side. What happened?

Have a look at your reflection in a metal spoon. What can you see? The shape of the spoon causes light to bounce off it in different ways. This is why your reflection probably looks a little strange. It might stretch or squash your reflection, or even turn it upside down.

Fun house mirrors can make you look very strange because their shape bends the light.

# COLOURS AND THE VISIBLE LIGHT SPECTRUM

## WHAT COLOUR IS LIGHT?

Natural light, such as sunlight, is actually made up of seven different colours: red, orange, yellow, green, blue, indigo and violet. When natural light passes through a **prism**, it splits the light into these colours. We call this the visible light **spectrum**.

A prism is a special triangular shape made of glass that can separate light into all the colours of the rainbow.

# HAVE YOU EVER WONDERED WHY GRASS IS GREEN?

When the light hits the grass, only the green light is reflected off.

When light bounces off grass, only the green light is reflected. Remember, natural light is made up of seven colours. All the other colours are not reflected by the grass, so we don't see them.

So, green grass reflects the green part of light. A red apple reflects the red part of the light. What happens to the light when it hits this penguin? There isn't any black or white in the visible light spectrum.

When light hits something that is black, none of the colours of the spectrum bounce off. They all get **absorbed**. When the light hits something that is white, all of the colours of the spectrum bounce off.

No light is reflected off a black surface.

When all the colours of the spectrum mix, they make white.

# DISAPPEARING COLOURS

## HOW DO YOU MAKE A RAINBOW DISAPPEAR?

You will need an adult to help you with this.

**1:** Draw a circle on a piece of card.

**2:** Split the circle into seven equal sections and colour them in with the seven colours of the rainbow.

**3:** Cut out your circle and push a pencil through the middle.

**4:** Now spin your rainbow spinning top.

**5:** What happens to the colours?

Make sure you spin it on a flat surface.

18

When you spin the rainbow spinning top, all the colours of the light spectrum mix together when you see them. Just like when light bounces off something white, all of the colours are reflected into your eyes at once.

# RAINBOWS

Rainbows are amazing, but we don't see them in the sky all of the time. We only see them when the Sun shines through the rain.

The raindrops work just like hundreds of little prisms. They split the light into the seven colours of the spectrum over and over in the sky. When this happens, we see a rainbow.

You might spot rainbows in some unusual places on a sunny day.

# MAKE A RAINBOW

## DO YOU KNOW HOW TO MAKE A RAINBOW?

To make a rainbow at home, all you need is sunlight, a large bowl half filled with water, a small mirror and a piece of white paper.

**1:** Place the bowl of water in the sunlight.

**2:** Now hold the mirror in the water so it is half in.

**3:** Move the mirror around until it reflects the sunlight onto the white paper. What can you see?

There are lots of ways to make a rainbow. See if you can find some more.

You should be able to see a rainbow on your piece of paper. Don't worry if you can't – try moving the mirror around a bit more until the rainbow appears. What happens if you move the paper closer to the mirror?

# GLOSSARY

| | |
|---|---|
| **absorbed** | has taken in or soaked up |
| **invented** | when something new is made |
| **opaque** | does not let light through |
| **prism** | a transparent object that bends the light that passes through it |
| **spectrum** | a scale, often with extremes at each end |
| **transparent** | a material that lets light pass through it, causing it to be see-through |

# INDEX

24